QUICK MEALS

Michelle Berriedale Johnson

CHANCELLOR PRESS

CONTENTS

First published in Great Britain in 1980
This edition published in 1994 by Chancellor Press
an imprint of Reed Consumer Books Limited
Michelin House, 81 Fulham Road, London SW3 6RB
and Auckland, Melbourne, Singapore and Toronto

Reprinted 1994

Copyright © 1980 Reed International Books Limited

ISBN 1 85152 510 6

A CIP catalogue record for this book is available from the British Library

Produced by Mandarin Offset
Printed and bound in China

INTRODUCTION

Quick Meals is designed especially for those whose time is limited but who, none the less, like to serve appetizing food. Accordingly, no recipe in the book should take more than 45 minutes to prepare and cook; many will take far less.

Recipes are provided to suit every occasion and everyone's pocket – from a celebration dinner of fillet steak to a quick cheese snack.

To keep preparation time to a minimum, packaged, canned and frozen foods are used in many recipes. Of course, you are not obliged to take the short cuts – use fresh meat and vegetables rather than canned, if you have the extra time needed to prepare them. Having said that, rest assured that the convenience foods used in these recipes are of such high quality that none of the dishes will taste packaged. On the contrary, your family and friends will be impressed by your culinary expertise and speed!

NOTES

Standard spoon measurements are used in all recipes
1 tablespoon = one 15 ml spoon
1 teaspoon   = one 5 ml spoon
All spoon measures are level.

Fresh herbs are used unless otherwise stated. If unobtainable substitute a bouquet garni of the equivalent dried herbs, or use dried herbs instead but halve the quantities stated.

Use freshly ground black pepper where pepper is specified.

Ovens should be preheated to the specified temperature.

For all recipes, quantities are given in both metric and imperial measures. Follow either set but not a mixture of both, because they are not inter-changeable.

Spinach Consommé

2 x 411 g (14½ oz)
  cans consommé
2 x 198 g (7 oz)
  cans spinach purée
200 ml (⅓ pint) dry
  sherry
pepper

Place the consommé, spinach purée and sherry in a pan and heat gently to just below boiling point.

Sprinkle with pepper to taste before serving.

Serves 4 to 6

Georgian Peanut Soup

2 x 283 g (10 oz)
   cans cream of
   chicken soup
50 g (2 oz) salted
   peanuts, finely
   chopped
150 ml (5 fl oz)
   single cream
120 ml (4 fl oz) dry
   sherry

Pour the soup into a pan, add the peanuts and heat gently. Do not boil.

When hot, stir in the cream and sherry and heat gently for 2 minutes.

Serve with toasted slices of French bread.

Serves 4

Cream of Pea and Ham Soup

1 x 600 ml (1 pint)
  packet thick green
  pea soup mix
600 ml (1 pint) milk
450 ml (¾ pint)
  water
125 g (4 oz) cooked
  ham, finely
  chopped
50 g (2 oz) frozen
  peas
175 ml (6 fl oz)
  natural low-fat
  yogurt
pepper

Place the powdered soup mix in a
pan and gradually stir in the milk
and water. Bring slowly to the boil,
stirring constantly, then add the ham
and peas. Cover and simmer for
20 minutes, stirring frequently.

Just before serving, stir in the
yogurt and pepper to taste. Serve hot
with crusty French bread.

Serves 4 to 6

Cream of Carrot Soup

2 x 397 g (14 oz)
  cans carrots
2 onions, chopped
50 g (2 oz) butter
50 g (2 oz) fresh
  white breadcrumbs
600 ml (1 pint) milk
salt and pepper
chopped parsley to
  garnish

Put the carrots, with their juice, the
onions, butter and breadcrumbs in a
saucepan. Add the milk and bring to
the boil. Cover and simmer for
5 minutes.

Rub through a sieve or work in an
electric blender until smooth. Add
salt and pepper to taste.

Reheat gently before serving,
garnished with parsley.

Serves 4 to 6

Tomato and Yogurt Soup

2 x 397 g (14 oz)
  cans tomatoes
2 cloves garlic,
  chopped
juice of 1 lemon
1 tablespoon sugar
1 tablespoon Worces-
  tershire sauce
400 ml (14 fl oz)
  natural low-fat
  yogurt
salt and pepper

Put the tomatoes, with their juice,
the garlic, lemon juice, sugar and
Worcestershire sauce in an electric
blender and work for about
3 minutes, until smooth.

Stir in the yogurt and add salt and
pepper to taste. Chill for at least
4 hours.

Serves 4 to 6

Celery and Onion Soup

1 x 524 g (18½ oz)
  can celery hearts
1 x 425 g (15 oz)
  can red kidney
  beans
1 x 425 g (15 oz)
  can French onion
  soup
300 ml (½ pint)
  water
150 ml (¼ pint)
  medium sherry
salt and pepper
grated Parmesan
  cheese to serve

Drain and chop the celery hearts, reserving the liquid. Drain the kidney beans.

Put the onion soup, celery hearts with their liquid, kidney beans, water and sherry in a saucepan. Heat to just below boiling point and add salt and pepper to taste.

Pour into individual soup bowls and sprinkle with Parmesan cheese to serve.

Serves 4 to 6

Vichysoisse

50 g (2 oz) butter
3 small leeks, thinly
  sliced
1 x 539 g (19 oz)
  can new potatoes,
  drained and
  chopped
600 ml (1 pint) milk
284 ml (10 fl oz)
  single cream
salt and white pepper
3 tablespoons
  chopped chives

Melt the butter in a saucepan, add the leeks and cook gently for about 15 minutes until soft.

Put the leeks, potatoes and milk in an electric blender and work until smooth. Stir in the cream and season with salt and pepper to taste. Stir in 2 tablespoons of the chives. Chill for at least 1 hour.

Sprinkle with the remaining chives before serving.

Serves 4

Cucumber and Prawn Soup

1 large cucumber
salt and pepper
300 ml (½ pint)
  natural low-fat
  yogurt
6 tablespoons lemon
  juice
250 ml (8 fl oz)
  single cream
2 tablespoons
  chopped chives
125 g (4 oz) shelled
  prawns

Grate the unpeeled cucumber into a bowl and sprinkle lightly with salt. Leave for 15 minutes.

Mix the yogurt, lemon juice and cream together and add to the cucumber. Stir in the chives, prawns and salt and pepper to taste.

Chill the soup for at least 1 hour before serving.

Serves 4

Creamed Mushrooms on Toast

50 g (2 oz) butter
1 small onion, finely
  chopped
juice of 1 lemon
250 g (8 oz) button
  mushrooms, sliced
4 teaspoons cornflour
350 ml (12 fl oz)
  single cream
2 teaspoons curry
  paste
salt and pepper
4 slices wholemeal
  bread, toasted and
  buttered
chopped parsley to
  garnish

Melt the butter in a frying pan, add the onion and fry gently until soft. Add the lemon juice and mushrooms and fry gently for 3 minutes.

Stir in the cornflour and cook, stirring, for 2 minutes. Gradually add the cream and cook gently, without boiling, until thickened. Add the curry paste with salt and pepper to taste.

Divide the mixture between the hot toast slices. Garnish with parsley and serve immediately.

Serves 4

Roe-Stuffed Baked Tomatoes

40 g (1 1/2 oz) butter
1 small onion, finely
  chopped
50 g (2 oz) fresh
  white breadcrumbs
1 x 99 g (3 1/2 oz)
  can smoked cod's
  roe
grated rind of 1/2
  lemon
salt and pepper
cayenne pepper
4 large tomatoes,
  halved, seeded and
  drained
2-3 tablespoons dry
  white wine
black olives to
  garnish

Melt 25 g (1 oz) of the butter in a frying pan, add the onion and fry until soft. Add the breadcrumbs and fry until golden. Keep 4 teaspoons of the mixture on one side.

Break up the cod's roe and stir into the breadcrumb mixture with the lemon rind. Season with salt, pepper and cayenne to taste.

Fill the tomato halves with the cod's roe mixture. Spoon the wine over the filling. Sprinkle with the reserved breadcrumb mixture and dot with the remaining butter.

Cook in a preheated moderate oven, 180°C (350°F), Gas Mark 4, for 15 to 20 minutes until the tomatoes are just tender. Serve hot, garnished with olives.

Serves 4

Mushroom and Emmenthal Salad

125 g (4 oz)
  Emmenthal cheese
250 g (8 oz) button
  mushrooms, sliced
250 ml (8 fl oz)
  single cream
juice of 2 lemons
salt and pepper
chopped parsley to
  garnish

Cut the cheese into thin strips and mix with the mushrooms and cream.
  Add the lemon juice and salt and pepper to taste; toss well.
  Spoon into a serving dish and sprinkle with parsley.
Serves 4

Spinach and Cream Cheese Pâté

250 g (8 oz) cream
  cheese
125 g (4 oz) frozen
  chopped spinach,
  thawed
few drops of Tabasco
  sauce
juice of 1/2 lemon
grated nutmeg
salt and pepper
4 lemon twists to
  garnish

Beat the cream cheese until soft. Drain the spinach thoroughly, then gradually add to the cream cheese, beating constantly.
  Add the Tabasco, lemon juice and nutmeg, salt and pepper to taste. Continue beating until the pâté is thoroughly blended. Spoon into individual dishes and chill well.
  Garnish each portion with a lemon twist. Serve with buttered wholemeal toast.
Serves 4
NOTE: Cooked fresh, or canned spinach may be used.

Sardine Eggs

4 hard-boiled eggs
1 x 120 g (4 1/2 oz)
  can sardines in oil
1 tablespoon fresh
  white breadcrumbs
2 tablespoons
  mayonnaise
1 tablespoon lemon
  juice
salt and pepper
chopped parsley to
  garnish

Cut the eggs in half lengthways and remove the yolks. Drain the sardines, discard any bones and chop finely.
  Mash the egg yolks, then mix with the sardines, breadcrumbs, mayonnaise and lemon juice. Season with salt and pepper to taste and beat until thoroughly blended. Pile the mixture into the egg white halves.
  Garnish with parsley and serve with buttered wholemeal bread.
Serves 4

Chicken and Walnut Pâté

175 g (6 oz) liver
  sausage
1 clove garlic,
  crushed
3 tablespoons
  medium sherry
125 g (4 oz) cooked
  chicken, chopped
50 g (2 oz) walnuts,
  roughly chopped
pepper
parsley sprigs to
  garnish

Mash the liver sausage thoroughly
with the garlic and sherry until
smooth.

Add the chicken, walnuts and
pepper to taste. Spoon into
individual dishes and garnish with
parsley.

Serve with buttered wholemeal
toast.

Serves 4

Smoked Mackerel Pâté

150 g (5 oz) butter
1 teaspoon creamed
   horseradish
250 g (8 oz) frozen
   smoked mackerel
   fillet, thawed
juice of 1 lemon
pinch of cayenne
   pepper
salt and pepper
lemon twists to
   garnish

Cream the butter with the horseradish until very soft. Remove the skin from the mackerel, flake and add to the butter. Beat to a fairly smooth paste. Add the lemon juice, cayenne and salt and pepper to taste.

Pile the mixture into a small tureen and garnish with lemon twists. Serve with thin slices of buttered toast.

Serves 4

Artichoke Heart and Bacon Salad

2 x 397 g (14 oz)
  cans artichoke
  hearts, drained
4 tablespoons French
  dressing
50 g (2 oz) lean
  thick bacon rashers

Toss the artichoke hearts in the French dressing and arrange in a serving dish.

Cut the bacon into strips. Place a frying pan over moderate heat, add the bacon and fry in its own fat until crisp.

Sprinkle the bacon over the salad. Serve immediately.
Serves 4

Avocado with Pears and Black Olives

2 avocados
2 tablespoons lemon
   juice
6 large black olives
1 ½ tablespoons
   mayonnaise
1 x 212 g (7½ oz)
   can pear quarters,
   drained and diced
salt and pepper

Halve the avocados, discard the
stones and rub with a little of the
lemon juice to prevent discoloration.

Halve the olives and discard the
stones. Set aside 4 halves for garnish;
chop the remainder.

Mix the mayonnaise and
remaining lemon juice together in a
bowl. Add the pears, chopped olives,
and salt and pepper to taste.

Pile the mixture into the avocado
halves. Garnish each portion with an
olive half.

Serves 4

Melon and Anchovy Salad

1 medium melon
1 x 49 g (1¾ oz)
  can anchovy fillets
juice of 1 lemon
juice of 1 orange
1 teaspoon caster
  sugar (optional)
watercress sprigs to
  garnish

Halve the melon and discard the seeds. Scoop the flesh into a serving dish, using a melon baller (or cut into cubes).

Drain the anchovy fillets, reserving 1 tablespoon of the oil. Cut the anchovies into short slivers and add to the melon.

Mix the lemon and orange juice with the reserved anchovy oil and pour over the salad. Add sugar to taste. Chill before serving, garnished with watercress.

Serves 4

Eggs Mimosa

4 hard-boiled eggs
1 x 42 g (1½ oz)
   can lumpfish
   caviar
6-8 tablespoons
   mayonnaise
1 small lettuce to
   garnish

Halve the eggs lengthways, remove the yolks and arrange the whites in a serving dish. Fill the egg white hollows with the caviar.

Rub the yolks through a sieve and spoon over the caviar, reserving 1 tablespoon for garnish.

Spoon the mayonnaise over the eggs, covering them completely.

Garnish with the reserved egg yolk and lettuce. Serve with thin slices of brown bread.

Serves 4

VARIATION: Replace the caviar with 125 g (4 oz) lumpfish cod's roe, 150 g (5 oz) natural low–fat yogurt and the juice of 1 lemon. Mash these ingredients together, adding salt and pepper to taste, and use to fill the egg whites.

Prawn-Stuffed Cucumbers

1 large cucumber, cut
 into 8 pieces
75 g (3 oz) cream
 cheese
2 tablespoons lemon
 juice
125 g (4 oz) prawns
1 x 99 g (3½ oz)
 can pimentos,
 drained and
 chopped
8 mint leaves,
 chopped
salt and pepper
paprika

Hollow out the centre of each
cucumber section to form cup shapes
and stand upright on a serving dish.
   Mix the cream cheese and lemon
juice together. Set aside 8 prawns for
garnish. Add the remainder to the
cheese mixture, with the pimentos
and mint. Season with salt, pepper
and paprika to taste; mix well.
   Pile the filling into the cucumber
cups and garnish with the reserved
prawns. Serve with thin slices of
buttered brown bread.
Serves 4

Asparagus Gratinée

4 slices wholemeal
bread, toasted and
buttered
1 x 340 g (12 oz)
can asparagus
spears, drained
50 g (2 oz) Cheddar
cheese, grated
pepper

Arrange the toast in a shallow
flameproof dish. Divide the
asparagus spears equally between the
toast slices and sprinkle with the
cheese.

Place under a preheated hot grill
for about 4 minutes, until the cheese
has melted and is lightly browned.
Sprinkle with pepper to taste and
serve immediately.

Serves 4

Pork Chops with Mustard Sauce

25 g (1 oz) butter
1 onion, finely sliced
1 tablespoon flour
salt and pepper
4 pork chops
120 ml (4 fl oz)
  medium sherry
175 ml (6 fl oz)
  chicken stock
2 tablespoons light
  French mustard

Melt the butter in a flameproof casserole, add the onion and fry until soft. Remove with a slotted spoon and set aside.

Season the flour with salt and pepper and use to coat the chops. Add to the casserole and fry briskly until browned on both sides.

Return the onion to the casserole and add the sherry and stock. Cover and simmer for 30 minutes, or until the chops are cooked.

Transfer the chops to a warmed serving dish, using a slotted spoon. Add the mustard to the sauce in the casserole, stir well and check the seasoning. Pour over the chops and serve immediately.

Serves 4

Pork Fillet with Plums

2 tablespoons plain
 flour
salt and pepper
500 g (1 lb) pork
 fillet, cut into 4
 pieces
50 g (2 oz) butter
1 x 567 g (20 oz)
 can Victoria
 plums, drained
 and stoned
1/4 teaspoon ground
 cinnamon
150 ml (1/4 pint) red
 wine
chopped parsley to
 garnish

Season the flour with salt and pepper and use to coat the pork.

Melt the butter in a frying pan, add the pork and fry until golden brown on both sides. Transfer to a casserole.

Mash the plums to a coarse purée. Stir in the cinnamon and wine and pour over the pork. Cover and cook in a preheated moderate oven, 180°C (350°F), Gas Mark 4, for 30 minutes.

Serve hot, garnished with parsley.

Serves 4

Barbecued Spare Ribs

1 kg (2 lb) pork
   spare ribs
5 tablespoons tomato
   ketchup
2 tablespoons clear
   honey
3 tablespoons soy
   sauce
3 tablespoons wine
   vinegar
1 ½ teaspoons tomato
   purée
1 teaspoon salt
300 ml (½ pint)
   stock
TO GARNISH:
1-2 spring onions,
   (green part only),
   finely chopped

Place the spare ribs in a roasting pan.
Mix together the ketchup, honey,
soy sauce, vinegar, tomato purée, salt
and stock and pour over the ribs. If
time, marinate for 2 to 3 hours.
Cook in a preheated hot oven, 220°C
(425°F), Gas Mark 7, for 15 minutes.

Transfer the spare ribs to a
roasting rack. Lower the oven
temperature to moderately hot,
190°C (375°F), Gas Mark 5, and cook
the spare ribs for a further
30 minutes until brown and crisp.

Meanwhile, place the roasting pan
over a moderate heat and boil the
cooking liquor until reduced to a
thick sauce.

Arrange the spare ribs on a serving
dish and pour over the sauce.
Garnish with the spring onion. Serve
with plain boiled rice.
Serves 4

26

Frankfurter and Bean Hot Pot

25 g (1 oz) butter
1 large onion,
   chopped
2 bacon rashers,
   derinded and
   chopped
4 frankfurters, diced
125 g (4 oz) garlic
   sausage, diced
1 tablespoon capers,
   chopped
2 x 425 g (15 oz)
   cans red kidney
   beans, drained
150 ml (¼ pint)
   light stock
salt and pepper
2 tablespoons
   chopped parsley

Melt the butter in a flameproof casserole, add the onion and bacon and fry gently until soft. Add the frankfurters, garlic sausage, capers and kidney beans. Mix well.

Stir in the stock. Cover and cook in a preheated moderate oven, 180°C (350°F), Gas Mark 4, for 20 minutes.

Check the seasoning and stir in the parsley. Serve immediately, accompanied by crusty French bread.
Serves 4

Tyrolean Veal with Sour Cream

2 tablespoons plain
  flour
salt and pepper
4 veal escalopes
50 g (2 oz) butter
1 small onion, finely
  chopped
2 tablespoons capers,
  with their vinegar
200 ml (1/3 pint)
  water
5 tablespoons fresh
  sour cream
chopped parsley to
  garnish

Season half the flour with salt and
pepper and use to coat the escalopes.

Melt half the butter in a frying
pan, add the veal and fry gently for
about 5 minutes on each side until
tender and golden. Remove and set
aside.

Melt the remaining butter in the
pan, add the onion and fry until soft.
Add the remaining flour and cook,
stirring, for 1 to 2 minutes.

Add the capers in their vinegar and
the water and cook until the sauce
thickens. Stir in the sour cream.
Return the veal to the pan and heat
through gently.

Sprinkle with parsley and serve
with plain boiled rice.

Serves 4

Veal Stroganoff

4 veal escalopes
50 g (2 oz) butter
1 onion, sliced
125 g (4 oz) button
  mushrooms, sliced
1-2 tablespoons
  tomato purée
1 tablespoon plain
  flour
142 ml (5 fl oz)
  fresh sour cream
salt and pepper
1-2 tablespoons
  lemon juice
watercress sprigs to
  garnish

Beat the escalopes until thin, then cut into short strips.

Melt half the butter in a frying pan, add the onion and mushrooms and fry until soft. Stir in the tomato purée and flour. Cook, stirring, over low heat for 2 to 3 minutes. Remove from the heat.

Melt the remaining butter in a clean pan, add the veal and fry over high heat, turning, until evenly browned. Add the meat to the sauce and stir well. Add the cream, salt, pepper and lemon juice to taste.

Garnish with watercress. Serve immediately, with buttered noodles or plain boiled rice.

Serves 4

Lamb and Apple Pie

250 g (8 oz) cooked
   lamb, finely
   chopped
250 g (8 oz) cooked
   ham, finely
   chopped
1 large cooking
   apple, peeled,
   cored and diced
1 large onion,
   chopped
salt and pepper
1 teaspoon chopped
   rosemary
200 ml (⅓ pint)
   chicken stock
200 ml (⅓ pint)
   cider
1 x 212 g (7½ oz)
   packet frozen
   shortcrust pastry,
   thawed
beaten egg to glaze

Place the lamb, ham, apple and onion in a 900 ml (1½ pint) pie dish, mix well and sprinkle with salt and pepper to taste and the rosemary. Pour over the stock and cider.

Roll out the pastry on a lightly floured board to a round slightly larger than the dish. Cut off a 2.5 cm (1 inch) strip all round, dampen and place along the edge of the dish.

Dampen the pastry strip and put the pastry lid in position. Knock up and flute the edges of the pastry. Cut a slit in the top and decorate with pastry leaves cut from any trimmings.

Brush with beaten egg and bake in a preheated moderately hot oven, 190°C (375°F), Gas Mark 5, for 35 minutes or until the pastry is cooked and golden.
Serves 4

Barbecued Lamb Cutlets

4 drops Tabasco
   sauce
2 teaspoons chilli
   powder
2 teaspoons salt
1 1/2 tablespoons soft
   brown sugar
1 1/2 tablespoons
   Worcestershire
   sauce
2 tablespoons tomato
   ketchup
1 1/2 tablespoons wine
   vinegar
4 tablespoons water
8 lamb cutlets,
   trimmed

Mix the Tabasco, chilli powder, salt and brown sugar together in a large dish. Gradually stir in the Worcestershire sauce, tomato ketchup, vinegar and water. Add the cutlets and turn to coat thoroughly. Leave to marinate for 4 hours.

Transfer the cutlets to a grill rack and brush with the marinade. Cook under a preheated hot grill for 5 to 10 minutes on each side, depending on the thickness of the cutlets, basting frequently with the marinade.

Serve immediately with plain boiled rice or buttered noodles.
Serves 4

London Pie

500 g (1 lb) minced
  beef
2 onions, chopped
50 g (2 oz) sultanas
2 cooking apples,
  peeled, cored and
  chopped
2 tablespoons tomato
  purée
4 tablespoons beef
  stock
salt and pepper
1 x 70 g (2½ oz)
  packet instant
  mashed potato
150 ml (¼ pint)
  milk
150 ml (¼ pint)
  water
50 g (2 oz) Cheddar
  cheese, grated
parsley sprigs to
  garnish

Mix together the beef, onions,
sultanas and apples in a casserole.
Blend the tomato purée with the
stock and add to the beef mixture.
Season with salt and pepper to taste.

Cover with foil and cook in a
preheated moderate oven, 180°C
(350°F), Gas Mark 4, for 30 minutes.

Make up the potato, using the
milk and water, as directed on the
packet. Spoon over the top of the
pie. Sprinkle with cheese and return
to the oven for about 15 minutes,
until the cheese is melted and
browned.

Garnish with parsley and serve
immediately.
Serves 4

Chilli con Carne

50 g (2 oz) butter
2 large onions, finely
  chopped
2 cloves garlic,
  crushed
500 g (1 lb) minced
  beef
2 teaspoons chilli
  powder
4 teaspoons cumin
  powder
1 x 65 g (2¼ oz)
  can tomato purée
2 x 425 g (15 oz)
  cans red kidney
  beans, drained
300 ml (½ pint) beef
  stock
salt and pepper
chopped parsley to
  garnish

Melt the butter in a flameproof
casserole. Add the onions and garlic
and fry gently for 5 minutes until
golden. Stir in the beef and cook,
stirring, for 10 minutes.

Mix together the chilli powder,
cumin and tomato purée and stir into
the beef. Add the kidney beans, stock
and salt and pepper to taste.

Cover and cook in a preheated
moderate oven, 180°C (350°F), Gas
Mark 4, for 25 minutes.

Sprinkle with chopped parsley and
serve hot, with plain boiled rice or
crusty French bread.
Serves 4

Liver and Bacon with Apple Rings

50 g (2 oz) butter
2 large cooking
    apples, peeled,
    cored and cut into
    thick rings
500 g (1 lb) calves'
    liver, sliced
4 rashers lean bacon,
    derinded

Melt half the butter in a frying pan, add the apple rings and fry gently until soft. Transfer to a warmed dish; keep hot.

Melt the remaining butter in the pan, add the liver and fry gently for about 2 minutes on each side until tender.

Meanwhile, cook the bacon under a preheated medium grill until crisp.

Transfer the liver to a warmed serving dish. Arrange the apple rings on top and the bacon around the edge. Serve immediately.

Serves 4

Steak au Poivre

1-2 tablespoons black
  peppercorns
4 fillet or entrecôte
  steaks
50 g (2 oz) butter
2 tablespoons
  brandy, warmed
250 ml (8 fl oz)
  single cream
salt

Crush the peppercorns and press them into both sides of the steaks. Leave to stand for 15 minutes.

Melt the butter in a heavy pan and fry the steaks quickly for 2 minutes on each side. Lower the heat and cook for a further 3 to 7 minutes on each side, until cooked to taste. Transfer to a warmed serving dish and keep hot.

Add the brandy to the juices in the pan and ignite. When the flames have died down, stir in the cream. Cook briskly for 2 minutes, stirring constantly. Add salt to taste. Pour the sauce over the steaks and serve immediately.

Serves 4

NOTE: If available, use green peppercorns instead of black ones for a more subtle flavour.

Roast Beef Salad with Sour Cream and Olives

500 g (1 lb) rare
  roast beef, thickly
  sliced
175 ml (6 fl oz)
  fresh sour cream
juice of 1 lemon
125 g (4 oz) black
  olives, halved and
  stoned

Cut the beef slices into strips and place in a serving dish. Mix together the sour cream and lemon juice. Add half the olives to the beef slices and spoon over the cream.

Garnish with the remaining olives. Serve with jacket potatoes and side salads of choice.

Serves 4

Cold Tongue Giardinera

125 g (4 oz) frozen
    mixed vegetables,
    lightly cooked
2 pickled onions,
    chopped
2 gherkins, chopped
6 stuffed olives,
    sliced
50 g (2 oz) capers,
    chopped
4 tablespoons French
    dressing
1 tablespoon vinegar
    (from the pickles)
350 g (12 oz) cooked
    tongue, thinly
    sliced
4 hard-boiled eggs,
    sliced
chopped parsley to
    garnish

Put the vegetables in a bowl with the pickled onions, gherkins, olives, capers, French dressing and pickling vinegar. Leave to marinate for 4 hours.

Arrange the tongue and egg slices on a serving dish and spoon over the vegetable mixture. Garnish with parsley. Serve cold, with crusty bread rolls.

Serves 4

Spiced Country Chicken

4 chicken portions
2 tablespoons plain
   flour
25 g (1 oz) butter
1 onion, finely
   chopped
1 clove garlic,
   crushed
1 green pepper,
   cored, seeded and
   chopped
2 teaspoons curry
   powder
1 teaspoon chopped
   thyme
1 x 227 g (8 oz) can
   tomatoes
2 tablespoons sweet
   white vermouth
salt and pepper
50 g (2 oz) raisins

Coat the chicken portions with flour. Melt the butter in a large pan, add the chicken and fry briskly until golden all over. Remove from the pan and set aside.

Add the onion, garlic, green pepper, curry powder and thyme to the fat remaining in the pan and fry, stirring, for 5 minutes.

Add the tomatoes with their juice and the vermouth. Return the chicken to the pan and add salt and pepper to taste. Cover and cook for 20 minutes, or until the chicken is tender.

Stir in the raisins and serve hot, with jacket potatoes or plain boiled rice.

Serves 4

Chicken with Oranges and Almonds

50 g (2 oz) butter
50 g (2 oz) flaked
   almonds
4 chicken portions
salt and pepper
paprika
3 oranges
2 teaspoons caster
   sugar

Melt the butter in a pan, add the almonds and fry gently until golden. Remove with a slotted spoon and set aside.

Sprinkle the chicken with salt, pepper and paprika to taste. Add to the fat remaining in the pan and fry, turning, until golden all over. Cover and cook gently for 30 minutes, or until tender.

Meanwhile, squeeze the juice from two of the oranges. Carefully cut the third orange into segments, discarding all pith.

Transfer the chicken to a warmed serving dish and keep hot.

Add the orange juice, orange segments and sugar to the pan juices and boil rapidly for 2 minutes. Pour over the chicken. Sprinkle with the almonds and serve immediately.
Serves 4

Pineapple Chicken

4 chicken portions
1 onion, thinly sliced
1 teaspoon salt
1/4 teaspoon pepper
1/2 teaspoon dried
    rosemary
1/2 teaspoon ground
    ginger
pinch of paprika
1 x 539 g (19 oz)
    can unsweetened
    pineapple juice
chopped parsley to
    garnish

Put the chicken in a casserole dish. Sprinkle with the onion, salt, pepper, rosemary, ginger and paprika and pour over the pineapple juice.

Cook in a preheated moderate oven, 180°C (350°F), Gas Mark 4, for 45 minutes or until the chicken is cooked and browned on top. Serve hot, garnished with parsley.

Serves 4

Chicken and Walnut Salad

500 g (1 lb) cooked
  boned chicken
2 celery sticks,
  coarsely chopped
1 large dessert apple,
  cored and diced
50 g (2 oz) walnuts,
  roughly chopped
6 tablespoons
  mayonnaise
1-2 tablespoons
  single cream
  (optional)
watercress sprigs to
  garnish

Cut the chicken into pieces and place in a large bowl with the celery, apple and walnuts.

Thin the mayonnaise if necessary to give the consistency of thick cream, by adding a little single cream. Pour over the chicken and toss well until the ingredients are evenly coated.

Turn into a serving dish and garnish with watercress.

Serves 4

Seafood Curry

2 tablespoons oil
2 onions, chopped
½ red pepper, cored, seeded and chopped
2 celery sticks, chopped
50 g (2 oz) mushrooms, sliced
1½ tablespoons curry powder
½ teaspoon turmeric
½ teaspoon ground ginger
1 cooking apple, peeled, cored and diced
250 g (8 oz) haddock fillet
125 g (4 oz) prawns
50 g (2 oz) raisins
1 teaspoon Worcestershire sauce
2 teaspoons tomato purée
6 tablespoons white wine
6 tablespoons water
salt and pepper
2 tablespoons natural low-fat yogurt
juice of ½ lemon

Heat the oil in a large pan. Add the onions, pepper, celery and mushrooms and fry gently for 5 minutes. Add the curry powder, turmeric and ginger and cook, stirring, for 2 minutes.

Add the apple, haddock, prawns, raisins, Worcestershire sauce and tomato purée and stir well. Stir in the wine and water and season with salt and pepper to taste. Cover and simmer gently for 10 minutes.

Just before serving, stir in the yogurt and lemon juice. Serve with plain boiled rice.

Serves 4

Haddock and Egg Mornay

4 smoked haddock
   fillets, skinned
450 ml (¾ pint)
   milk
1 bouquet garni
4 eggs
40 g (1½ oz) butter
40 g (1½ oz) plain
   flour
75 g (3 oz) Cheddar
   cheese
pepper
parsley sprigs to
   garnish

Place the haddock in a pan with the milk and bouquet garni. Cook over low heat for 10 minutes or until tender. Transfer to a warmed serving dish, using a slotted spoon, and keep hot. Strain the milk and reserve.

Poach the eggs in simmering water for 4 to 5 minutes. Meanwhile, melt the butter in a pan. Stir in the flour and cook, stirring, for 2 minutes. Blend in the milk and simmer, stirring, until thickened. Stir in two-thirds of the cheese.

Using a slotted spoon, place a poached egg on each haddock fillet. Top with the cheese sauce and sprinkle with the remaining cheese and pepper to taste. Place under a preheated hot grill until lightly browned. Serve immediately, garnished with parsley.

Serves 4

Fish and Potato Pie

350 g (12 oz)
haddock or cod
fillet
1 x 212 g (7½ oz)
can button mush-
rooms, drained
1 x 227 g (8 oz) can
tomatoes
125 g (4 oz) prawns
1 x 300 ml (½ pint)
packet onion sauce
mix
200 ml (⅓ pint)
milk
150 ml (¼ pint)
white wine
1 x 70 g (2½ oz)
packet instant
mashed potato
6-7 tablespoons
water
salt and pepper
25 g (1 oz) butter
TO GARNISH:
tomato slices
parsley sprigs

Cut the fish fillets into large pieces and place in a casserole. Cover with the mushrooms and tomatoes and pour over a little of the tomato juice. Sprinkle the prawns on top.

Make up the onion sauce as directed on the packet, using 150 ml (¼ pint) of the milk and the wine. Pour over the prawns.

Make up the potato as directed on the packet, using the remaining milk and the water. Add salt and pepper to taste. Spoon over the fish mixture to cover completely. Dot with the butter.

Bake in a preheated moderate oven, 180°C (350°F), Gas Mark 4, for 30 minutes, until the top is golden brown. Serve hot, garnished with tomato and parsley.
Serves 4

Baked Trout

50 g (2 oz) butter
4 trout, cleaned
1 lemon, sliced
5 tablespoons dry
white wine
1 teaspoon dried
tarragon
salt and pepper
parsley sprigs to
garnish

Line a baking dish with a large piece of foil, allowing sufficient to hang over the sides. Spread the butter over the foil. Lay the trout in the dish and arrange the lemon slices on top.

Mix together the wine, tarragon and salt and pepper to taste and pour over the fish.

Fold the foil over the trout to make a parcel and fold the edges together to seal. Cook in a preheated moderate oven, 180°C (350°F), Gas Mark 4, for 30 minutes.

Transfer the trout to a warmed serving dish. Pour over the juices and garnish with parsley.
Serves 4

Pacific Tuna Pie

2 x 198 g (7 oz)
  cans tuna fish,
  drained and flaked
1 x 326 g (11½ oz)
  can sweetcorn,
  drained
1 x 113 g (4 oz)
  packet frozen peas
1 x 298 g (10½ oz)
  can condensed
  chicken soup
1 x 397 g (14 oz)
  can tomatoes,
  drained
75 g (3 oz) Cheddar
  cheese, grated
1 x 75 g (3 oz)
  packet potato
  crisps, crushed

Mix together the tuna, sweetcorn, peas and soup. Turn into a buttered casserole and cover with the tomatoes.

Mix together the cheese and crisps and sprinkle over the tomatoes. Cook in a preheated moderately hot oven, 190°C (375°F), Gas Mark 5, for 30 minutes, until the top is golden and bubbling.

Serve hot, with baked tomatoes if liked.

Serves 4

Cod in Caper Mayonnaise

4 cod fillets, skinned
salt and pepper
150 ml (¼ pint) dry
    white wine
½ lemon, sliced
6 tablespoons
    mayonnaise
4 tablespoons lemon
    juice
50 g (2 oz) capers,
    chopped

Place the fish in a frying pan and sprinkle with salt and pepper to taste. Add the wine and lemon slices, cover and simmer for 20 minutes.

Remove the fish from the pan, reserving 2 tablespoons of the cooking liquor, and leave to cool.

Mix together the mayonnaise, lemon juice and the reserved liquor. Stir in the capers.

Place the fish in a serving dish and top with the caper sauce. Serve cold.

Serves 4

Prawn and Artichoke Vol-au-Vents

1 x 300 ml (½ pint)
    packet onion sauce
    mix
150 ml (¼ pint)
    milk
150 ml (¼ pint) dry
    white wine
125 g (4 oz) frozen
    petit pois
1 x 397 g (14 oz)
    can artichoke
    hearts, drained and
    quartered
350 g (12 oz) frozen
    peeled prawns,
    thawed
2 tablespoons single
    cream
celery salt
white pepper
8 frozen vol-au-vent
    cases
parsley sprigs to
    garnish

Make up the sauce mix, following the directions on the packet, using the milk and wine. Add the petit pois, artichoke hearts and prawns. Simmer gently for 4 minutes.

Add the cream and season with celery salt and pepper to taste.

Cook the vol-au-vent cases from frozen, according to packet directions. Spoon in the prawn mixture and garnish with parsley. Serve immediately.

Serves 4

Plaice in Orange Mayonnaise

4 plaice, skinned and
    filleted
grated rind and juice
    of 2 oranges
juice of 1 lemon
salt and pepper
150 ml (¼ pint)
    mayonnaise
TO GARNISH:
anchovy fillets
orange segments

Sprinkle the fish with the rind and
juice of 1 orange, the lemon juice,
and salt and pepper to taste. Roll up
and place in a buttered ovenproof
dish. Cover and cook in a preheated
moderate oven, 180°C (350°F), Gas
Mark 4, for 20 minutes or until just
tender. Leave to cool.

Add the remaining grated orange
rind and juice to the mayonnaise and
mix well.

Place the fish in a serving dish and
pour over the mayonnaise. Garnish
with anchovy fillets and orange
segments. Serve cold.
Serves 4

Crunchy Salmon Salad

3 tablespoons
    mayonnaise
6 tablespoons lemon
    juice
2 x 205 g (7½ oz)
    cans red salmon
2 dessert apples, peeled,
    cored and diced
175 g (6 oz) salted
    peanuts, chopped
salt and pepper
1 lettuce

Mix the mayonnaise and lemon juice
together in a bowl. Drain the
salmon, flake and add to the
mayonnaise. Stir in the apples,
peanuts and salt and pepper to taste.

Line a serving dish with lettuce
leaves and pile the salmon mixture
into the centre.
Serves 4

Tuna and Bean Salad

1 x 99 g (3½ oz)
    and 1 x 198 g
    (7 oz) can tuna
    fish, drained and
    flaked
1 x 439 g (15½ oz)
    can butter beans,
    drained
4 tablespoons French
    dressing
chopped capers to
    garnish

Mix the tuna and butter beans
together. Pour over the French
dressing and toss well to coat.

Turn into a serving dish and
garnish with capers.
Serves 4

VEGETABLES & SALADS

Spinach with Onion and Bacon

2 tablespoons oil
4 bacon rashers,
    derinded and
    chopped
1 onion, chopped
1-2 garlic cloves,
    crushed
500 g (1 lb) spinach
    leaves
1 tablespoon lemon
    juice
salt and pepper

Heat the oil in a large pan. Add the bacon, onion and garlic and fry gently for 5 minutes.

Add the spinach, lemon juice and salt and pepper to taste. Fry gently for 3 to 5 minutes, stirring constantly, until the spinach is just tender. Serve immediately.

Serves 4

Celery with Walnuts

1 x 524 g (18½ oz)
  can celery hearts
25 g (1 oz) butter
25 g (1 oz) walnut
  pieces

Place the celery hearts, with their juice, in a saucepan over moderate heat. When hot, drain, place in a warmed serving dish and keep hot.

Melt the butter in a small pan, add the walnuts and fry until just beginning to brown. Spoon over the celery and serve immediately.

Serves 4

Mushroom and Onion Casserole

50 g (2 oz) butter
500 g (1 lb) onions, roughly chopped
500 g (1 lb) mushrooms, sliced
200 ml (⅓ pint) stock
2 tablespoons sherry
2 tablespoons lemon juice
salt and pepper
chopped parsley to garnish

Melt the butter in a flameproof casserole. Add the onions and fry gently for 10 minutes, until soft. Add the mushrooms, stock, sherry, lemon juice, and salt and pepper to taste.

Cover and cook in a preheated moderate oven, 180°C (350°F), Gas Mark 4, for 15 minutes. Serve hot, garnished with parsley.
Serves 4

Herb–Glazed Carrots

1 x 539 g (19 oz) can baby carrots
25 g (1 oz) butter
2 teaspoons sugar
6 mint leaves, finely chopped

Heat the carrots with their juice in a saucepan over moderate heat; drain.

Place the butter and sugar in a small pan. Heat gently, stirring, until dissolved, then add the mint. Add the carrots and toss well. Turn into a warmed serving dish. Serve hot.
Serves 4
NOTE: Frozen small whole carrots may be used instead of canned ones: Plunge 500 g (1 lb) frozen carrots into boiling salted water and cook for 5 to 10 minutes until tender.

Baked Onions

4 large or 8 medium onions, unpeeled
salt and pepper
chopped parsley to garnish

Cut a small piece off the root end of each onion. Cut off the tops and make 4 vertical slits through the skin from the top to the middle of each onion.

Place on a baking sheet and cook in a preheated moderate oven, 180°C (350°F), Gas Mark 4, for 30 to 45 minutes, depending on the size of the onions, until the centres are tender.

Remove the skins from the onions. Season with salt and pepper to taste and garnish with parsley. Serve hot.
Serves 4

Corn Fritters

1 x 326 g (11½ oz)
  can sweetcorn,
  drained
2 teaspoons soft
  brown sugar
3 eggs, beaten
50 g (2 oz) butter,
  melted
4 tablespoons grated
  Parmesan cheese
salt and pepper
oil for deep-frying
watercress sprigs to
  garnish

Put the sweetcorn in a bowl. Add the sugar, eggs, butter, cheese and salt and pepper to taste. Mix thoroughly.

Heat the oil in a deep-fat fryer to 180°C (350°F). Drop tablespoonfuls of the corn mixture into the hot oil and fry for about 4 minutes, until crisp and golden.

Remove with a slotted spoon, drain on kitchen paper and serve warm, garnished with watercress.

Serves 4

Crispy Corn Bake

25 g (1 oz) plain
    flour
2 eggs, beaten
25 g (1 oz) soft
    brown sugar
25 g (1 oz) butter,
    melted
6 tablespoons milk
salt and pepper
2 x 326 g (11¹/₂ oz)
    cans sweetcorn,
    drained
1 x 75 g (3 oz)
    packet potato
    crisps, crushed
parsley sprigs to
    garnish

Put the flour in a bowl and gradually add the eggs, sugar, butter and milk, beating constantly to give a smooth mixture. Season with salt and pepper to taste and stir in the sweetcorn.

Spoon the mixture into an ovenproof dish and sprinkle the crisps over the top.

Bake in a preheated moderately hot oven, 190°C (375°F), Gas Mark 5, for 35 minutes until golden and firm. Serve hot, garnished with parsley.

Serves 4

Braised Cabbage with Bacon

2 rashers back bacon,
    derinded and
    chopped
1 small white cabbage,
    roughly chopped
1 onion, chopped
6 tablespoons natural
    low-fat yogurt
6 tablespoons chicken
    stock
1 teaspoon paprika
salt and pepper

Place a frying pan over moderate heat, add the bacon and cook briskly until crisp. Transfer to an ovenproof dish and add the cabbage and onion.

Mix the yogurt and stock together with the paprika and salt and pepper to taste. Pour over the cabbage.

Cover and cook in a preheated moderate oven, 180°C (350°F), Gas Mark 4, for 40 minutes, stirring halfway through cooking.

Serves 4

Brussels Sprouts with Chestnuts

125 g (4 oz)
    chestnuts
1 x 454 g (1 lb)
    pack frozen
    Brussels sprouts
salt
25 g (1 oz) butter

Score the chestnuts around the middle and place on a baking sheet. Bake in a preheated moderate oven, 180°C (350°F), Gas Mark 4, for 10 minutes. When cool enough to handle, peel the chestnuts.

Cook the sprouts in boiling salted water for 3 to 5 minutes.

Meanwhile, melt the butter in a shallow pan. Add the chestnuts and fry briskly, turning, for 2 minutes.

Drain the sprouts and place in a serving dish. Add the chestnuts and butter. Serve immediately.

Serves 4

Potato and Cheese Pie

750 g (1 ½ lb) boiled
    potatoes, mashed
salt and pepper
grated nutmeg
50 g (2 oz) butter
75 g (3 oz) Cheddar
    cheese, grated
TO GARNISH:
tomato slices
parsley sprigs

Season the potato with salt, pepper and nutmeg to taste and beat in half the butter. Spread the mixture in a shallow ovenproof dish. Top with the cheese and remaining butter.

Cook in a preheated moderate oven, 180°C (350°F), Gas Mark 4, for 15 minutes, then place under a preheated hot grill for 3 minutes.

Sprinkle with pepper and garnish with tomato and parsley. Serve hot.

Serves 4

Carrot and Raisin Salad

500 g (1 lb) carrots,
  grated
75 g (3 oz) raisins
2 tablespoons soy
  sauce
chopped parsley to
  garnish

Put the carrot and raisins in a serving dish and mix well.

Sprinkle over the soy sauce and toss well. Garnish with chopped parsley.

Serves 4

NOTE: As a variation, replace half the carrots with coarsely grated white cabbage.

Tomatoes with Horseradish Mayonnaise

4 large tomatoes,
   sliced
3 tablespoons
   mayonnaise
1 tablespoon creamed
   horseradish
1-2 tablespoons
   single cream
   (optional)
chopped parsley to
   garnish

Arrange the tomatoes in a serving dish. Mix the mayonnaise with the horseradish, adding a little single cream if necessary to give the consistency of thick cream.

Spoon the dressing over the tomatoes and sprinkle with parsley.
Serves 4

Green and White Vegetable Salad

50 g (2 oz) frozen
  green peas, thawed
125 g (4 oz) white
  cabbage, thinly
  sliced
2 celery sticks,
  chopped
1 small green pepper,
  cored, seeded and
  chopped
½ onion or ½ leek,
  thinly sliced
125 g (4 oz)
  Brussels sprouts,
  quartered
125 g (4 oz) bean
  sprouts
4 tablespoons French
  dressing

Mix all the vegetables together in a salad bowl. Pour over the dressing and toss well. Serve immediately.
Serves 4

Cabbage Salad with Peanut Dressing

1 small white cabbage, finely sliced
125 g (4 oz) salted peanuts, chopped
2 red peppers, cored, seeded and finely chopped
1 teaspoon anchovy essence
1 tablespoon soy sauce
2 tablespoons lemon juice
1 teaspoon cayenne pepper
$\frac{1}{2}$ teaspoon salt
1 teaspoon soft brown sugar

Put the cabbage in a salad bowl. Combine the remaining ingredients to form a crunchy sauce. Spoon over the cabbage and serve immediately.
Serves 4

Beetroot and Orange Salad

2 large oranges
4 tablespoons French
  dressing
1 clove garlic, finely
  sliced (optional)
500 g (1 lb) cooked
  beetroot, sliced
watercress or mint
  sprigs to garnish

Grate the rind from one of the oranges and mix with the dressing. Add the garlic, if using. Peel and thinly slice both oranges, removing all pith.

Arrange the orange and beetroot slices in alternate layers in a serving dish. Pour the dressing over the top and garnish with watercress or mint sprigs. Chill before using.

Serves 4

Date and Nut Salad

175 g (6 oz) dates,
  stoned and halved
3 crisp dessert apples,
  cored and sliced
50 g (2 oz) walnut
  pieces
3 tablespoons lemon
  juice
150 ml (¼ pint)
  natural low-fat
  yogurt
salt

Put the dates, apples and walnuts in a
serving bowl.

Mix together the lemon juice and
yogurt. Add salt to taste. Pour over
the salad and toss well until the
ingredients are evenly coated.
Serves 4

SNACKS & SUPPER DISHES

Egg Florentine

750 g (1½ lb)
  frozen leaf
  spinach, thawed
  and well drained
50 g (2 oz) butter
grated nutmeg
salt and pepper
4 eggs
4 tablespoons grated
  Parmesan cheese

Place the spinach and half the butter in a large pan. Add nutmeg, salt and pepper to taste. Cook gently for 2 to 3 minutes until tender. Transfer to a shallow ovenproof dish.

Make 4 hollows in the spinach and carefully break an egg into each one. Sprinkle 1 tablespoon cheese over each egg and dot with the remaining butter.

Cook in a preheated moderate oven, 180°C (350°F), Gas Mark 4, for 15 minutes or until the eggs are cooked.

Sprinkle with pepper. Serve immediately, accompanied by wholemeal bread.

Serves 4

Curried Egg Salad

150 ml (¼ pint)
  mayonnaise
4 tablespoons double
  cream
1 tablespoon curry
  paste
salt and pepper
6 hard-boiled eggs,
  quartered
1 crisp lettuce
salad cress or
  watercress to
  garnish

Mix together the mayonnaise, cream and curry paste. Season with salt and pepper to taste. Carefully fold in the eggs.

Line a serving dish with the lettuce. Pile the egg mixture in the centre and garnish with cress or watercress.

Serves 4

English Rarebit

50 g (2 oz) butter
300 ml (½ pint) beer
350 g (12 oz)
  mature Cheddar
  cheese
1½ tablespoons
  cornflour
1½ tablespoons
  Meaux mustard
1 teaspoon anchovy
  essence
1 teaspoon
  Worcestershire
  sauce
salt and pepper
4 slices wholemeal
  bread, toasted and
  buttered
parsley sprigs to
  garnish

Melt the butter in a pan, add half the beer and the cheese. Heat gently until the cheese is melted.

Blend the cornflour with the remaining beer and add to the pan. Cook gently until the mixture thickens, then add the mustard, anchovy essence, Worcestershire sauce and salt to taste.

Arrange the toast slices in a shallow flameproof dish and pour over the cheese mixture. Place under a preheated hot grill for 3 to 4 minutes until golden and bubbling.

Sprinkle with pepper to taste and garnish with parsley. Serve immediately.
Serves 4

Creamy Herbed Noodles

500 g (1 lb) noodles
salt and pepper
50 g (2 oz) butter
1 small onion, finely
  chopped
1 clove garlic, crushed
284 ml (10 fl oz)
  single cream
250 ml (8 fl oz) dry
  white wine
2 tomatoes, skinned,
  seeded and
  chopped
1 teaspoon green
  peppercorns
  (optional)
2 tablespoons
  chopped chives
4 mint leaves,
  chopped
4 tablespoons grated
  Parmesan cheese

Cook the noodles in plenty of boiling salted water for 9 minutes or until al dente (cooked but still firm to the bite).

Meanwhile, melt the butter in a small pan, add the onion and garlic and fry gently until soft and translucent. Add the cream, wine, tomatoes and peppercorns, if using, and heat to just below boiling point. Simmer gently for 4 minutes.

Drain the noodles and place in a warmed serving dish. Add the chives and mint to the sauce. Check the seasoning, adding pepper if green peppercorns have not been used. Pour over the noodles. Sprinkle with the Parmesan cheese.
Serves 4

Egg and Onion Casserole

25 g (1 oz) butter
300 ml (½ pint)
   milk
2 small onions,
   finely chopped
1 x 300 ml (½ pint)
   packet onion sauce
   mix
4 hard-boiled eggs,
   roughly chopped
4 tablespoons fresh
   white breadcrumbs

Melt the butter in a pan, add the milk and onions and bring slowly to the boil. Lower the heat, cover and simmer for 4 minutes.

Cool slightly, then gradually stir into the onion sauce mix. Return to the heat and cook until thickened.

Stir in the egg, pour into a small casserole dish and cover with the breadcrumbs.

Place under a preheated hot grill for 3 minutes or until the crumbs are crisp and golden.

Serves 4

67

French Toasts with Bacon

8 rashers lean bacon,
   derinded
3 large eggs
4 tablespoons milk
salt and pepper
4 thick slices brown
   or white bread
25 g (1 oz) lard

Place a frying pan over low heat, add the bacon and fry gently in its own fat until quite crisp. Remove from the pan with a slotted spoon and keep warm.

Beat the eggs and milk together, with salt and pepper to taste. Place the bread in a shallow dish and pour over the egg mixture. Leave to soak for a few minutes.

Melt the lard in the frying pan. Transfer the bread slices to the hot fat, using a fish slice, and fry both sides until golden brown. Transfer to serving plates and arrange the bacon slices on top. Serve immediately.
Serves 4

Salmon Savoury

2 x 212 g (7½ oz)
cans salmon,
drained and
mashed
250 g (8 oz)
Cheddar cheese,
grated
4 tablespoons natural
low-fat yogurt
4 tablespoons lemon
juice
salt and pepper
paprika
4 eggs, beaten
4 slices wholemeal
bread, toasted and
buttered
lemon wedges to
serve

Mix the salmon with the cheese. Stir in the yogurt and lemon juice. Season with salt, pepper and paprika to taste. Beat until well mixed, then beat in the eggs.

Put the toast in a shallow flameproof dish and pile the salmon mixture on top. Place under a preheated low grill for 10 minutes or until the mixture is heated through, then increase the heat and grill for a further 5 minutes to brown the top. Serve immediately, with lemon wedges.

Serves 4

Smoked Haddock Soufflé Omelet

50 g (2 oz) butter
2 smoked haddock
  fillets, cooked and
  flaked
5 tablespoons single
  cream
4 tablespoons grated
  Parmesan cheese
salt and pepper
6 eggs, separated
parsley sprigs to
  garnish

Melt half the butter in a saucepan. Add the haddock, cream and half the cheese and heat gently until the cheese is melted.

Remove from the heat and season with salt and pepper to taste. Stir in the egg yolks. Whisk the egg whites until stiff and fold into the haddock mixture.

Melt the remaining butter in a large frying pan. When sizzling, pour in the omelet mixture. Cook gently for 2 to 3 minutes until set, drawing the cooked edges towards the centre with a fork.

Cut into quarters and turn out on to warmed serving plates. Sprinkle with the remaining cheese and garnish with parsley. Serve immediately.
Serves 4

Spanish Omelet

1 tablespoon oil
1 clove garlic, crushed
2 onions, sliced
125 g (4 oz)
  sweetcorn
1 x 99 g (3½ oz)
  can pimentos,
  drained and sliced
1 medium potato,
  boiled and diced
50 g (2 oz) frozen
  peas
50 g (2 oz) chorizo
  or garlic sausage,
  chopped
8 eggs
salt and pepper
2 tablespoons water
25 g (1 oz) butter
watercress sprigs to
  garnish

Heat the oil in a frying pan, add the garlic and onions and cook for 10 minutes until soft.

Mix the sweetcorn, pimentos, potato, peas and sausage together. Add the onion and garlic.

Beat the eggs together with salt and pepper to taste and the water. Stir in the vegetable mixture.

Melt the butter in a large frying pan. When sizzling, pour in the omelet mixture and cook briskly for 5 minutes or until set, drawing the cooked edges towards the centre during the first minute.

Cut into quarters and turn out onto warmed serving plates. Garnish with watercress and serve immediately.
Serves 4

Savoury Macaroni Cheese

500 g (1 lb)
    macaroni
salt
4 rashers bacon,
    derinded and
    chopped
2 onions, chopped
2 x 300 ml (½ pint)
    packets cheese
    sauce mix
600 ml (1 pint) milk
120 ml (4 fl oz)
    single cream
175 g (6 oz)
    Cheddar cheese,
    grated
1 x 397 g (14 oz)
    can tomatoes,
    drained and
    chopped
TO GARNISH:
tomato slices
parsley sprigs

Cook the macaroni in plenty of
boiling salted water for 12 minutes
or until *al dente* (cooked but still firm
to the bite).

Cook the bacon in a frying pan
over low heat until the fat runs. Add
the onions and fry gently for
5 minutes.

Make up the cheese sauce with the
milk as directed on the packet, then
add to the bacon and onions. Stir in
the cream and half the cheese. Cook
gently until the cheese is melted.

Drain the macaroni and add to the
sauce, with the tomatoes; mix well.

Turn into a shallow flameproof
dish and top with the remaining
cheese. Place under a preheated hot
grill for 10 minutes or until the top is
crisp and brown. Garnish with
tomato and parsley. Serve
immediately.
Serves 4

71

Beef and Onion Patties

½ x 70 g (2½ oz)
  packet instant
  mashed potato
5 tablespoons milk
5 tablespoons water
1 x 198 g (7 oz)
  corned beef
1 onion, finely
  chopped
50 g (2 oz) fresh
  white breadcrumbs
2 teaspoons Worces-
  tershire sauce
2 teaspoons French
  mustard
2 eggs, beaten
salt and pepper
2 tablespoons
  vegetable oil

Make up the potato as directed on
the packet, using the milk and water.
  Mash the corned beef with a fork.
Add the onion, potato, breadcrumbs,
Worcestershire sauce, mustard and
eggs. Beat until thoroughly mixed.
Season with salt and pepper to taste.
  Heat the oil in a frying pan and
add tablespoonfuls of the mixture.
Fry gently for about 5 minutes on
each side, until firm and golden.
Remove and drain on kitchen paper.
  Serve hot, accompanied by a crisp
green salad.
Serves 4

Ham and Mushroom Toasts

1 x 300 ml (½ pint)
  packet onion sauce
  mix
300 ml (½ pint)
  milk
350 g (12 oz) button
  mushrooms, sliced
125 g (4 oz) cooked
  ham, diced
120 ml (4 fl oz)
  natural low-fat
  yogurt
4 slices brown or
  white bread,
  toasted and
  buttered
pepper
parsley sprigs to
  garnish

Put the sauce mix in a pan, stir in the milk and heat gently until thickened.

Add the mushrooms and ham. Cover and simmer for 5 minutes or until the mushrooms are tender.

Remove from the heat and stir in the yogurt. Spoon over the toast slices and sprinkle with pepper to taste. Garnish with parsley and serve immediately.

Serves 4

NOTE: This recipe is equally delicious prepared with tongue instead of ham.

Savoury Onion Puffs

25 g (1 oz) butter
350 g (12 oz)
  onions, chopped
175 g (6 oz)
  potatoes, boiled
  and diced
1 x 300 ml (½ pint)
  packet onion sauce
  mix
200 ml (⅓ pint)
  milk
125 g (4 oz)
  Cheddar cheese,
  grated
salt and pepper
1 x 212 g (7½ oz)
  packet frozen puff
  pastry, thawed
beaten egg to glaze

Melt the butter in a pan, add the onions and cook gently for 5 minutes. Add the potatoes.

Make up the sauce mix with the milk, as directed on the packet. Stir into the onion mixture with the cheese and salt and pepper to taste. Cook for 3 minutes.

Roll out the pastry on a lightly floured board to a 30 cm (12 inch) square and cut into 4 squares. Place on a baking sheet.

Divide the onion mixture between the squares, placing it in the centre of each. Dampen the edges and fold the pastry over the filling to form triangular puffs. Press the edges together to seal, trim, knock up and flute. Brush the pastry with beaten egg.

Cook in a preheated hot oven, 220°C (425°F), Gas Mark 7, for 15 minutes until well risen and golden.
Serves 4

Tomato Fondue

50 g (2 oz) butter
1 small onion, finely
  chopped
2 cloves garlic,
  crushed
1 x 794 g (28 oz)
  can tomatoes
1 teaspoon dried
  oregano
1 teaspoon paprika
2 teaspoons dried
  basil
300 ml (½ pint) dry
  white wine
salt and pepper
500 g (1 lb) Cheddar
  cheese, grated
bread cubes to serve

Melt the butter in a fondue dish or flameproof casserole. Add the onion and garlic and fry until softened.

Drain the tomatoes thoroughly, then mash to a pulp. Add to the onion, with the oregano, paprika, basil and wine. Season with salt and pepper to taste. Cook gently for 10 minutes.

Gradually stir in the cheese and cook over a low heat until melted. Check the seasoning. Serve immediately with the bread cubes. Dip these into the hot fondue before eating.
Serves 4

Fried Apple and Cheese Sandwiches

2 dessert apples,
   peeled, cored and
   grated
125 g (4 oz)
   Cheddar cheese,
   grated
1 x 113 g (4 oz)
   packet cream
   cheese
2 drops of Tabasco
   sauce
salt and pepper
8 slices wholemeal
   bread, buttered
50 g (2 oz) butter

Place the apple, Cheddar, cream
cheese and Tabasco in a bowl. Mix
until thoroughly blended. Season
with salt and pepper to taste.

Divide the mixture between four
of the bread slices and spread evenly.
Cover with the remaining bread.

Melt half the butter in a frying
pan. Add two of the sandwiches and
fry gently on both sides until golden
and the cheese has melted slightly.
Repeat with the remaining butter
and sandwiches. Serve immediately.
Serves 4

Baked Cheese and Mustard Pudding

4 thick slices brown
   or white bread,
   crusts removed
50 g (2 oz) butter
1-2 tablespoons
   English mustard
175 g (6 oz)
   Cheddar cheese,
   grated
pepper
2 eggs
2 egg yolks
150 ml (¼ pint)
   chicken stock,
   cooled
tomato slices to
   garnish

Spread both sides of the bread thickly with the butter and mustard to taste.

Put 2 slices in a well buttered pie dish. Cover with half the cheese and sprinkle with a little pepper. Top with the remaining bread.

Beat together the eggs and egg yolks and stir in the stock. Pour over the bread and top with the remaining cheese.

Cook in a preheated moderately hot oven, 190°C (375°F), Gas Mark 5, for 25 to 30 minutes until golden.

Garnish with tomato slices and serve immediately.

Serves 4

Baked Eggs in Orange Potatoes

*1 x 70 g (2½ oz)
packet instant
mashed potato
150 ml (¼ pint)
milk
150 ml (¼ pint)
water
salt and pepper
½ small onion,
finely chopped
grated rind of
1 orange
2 egg yolks
2 slices cooked ham,
finely chopped
4 eggs
50 g (2 oz) Cheddar
cheese, grated
25 g (1 oz) butter
watercress sprigs to
garnish*

Make up the potato as directed on
the packet, using the milk and water.
Season liberally with salt and pepper
and beat in the onion, orange rind
and egg yolks.

Spread in a shallow ovenproof
dish and make 4 hollows in the
potato. Line each hollow with
chopped ham and carefully break an
egg into each one. Sprinkle the eggs
with cheese and dot with butter.

Sprinkle with pepper to taste and
bake in a preheated moderately hot
oven, 190°C (375°F), Gas Mark 5, for
20 minutes, or until the eggs are
firm.

Garnish with watercress and serve
immediately.
Serves 4

77

DESSERTS

Yogurt Cheesecake

175 g (6 oz) cream
  cheese
150 g (5 oz) natural
  low-fat yogurt
2 drops vanilla
  essence
2 tablespoons thick
  honey
2 teaspoons lemon
  juice
1 x 15-18 cm
  (6-7 inch) flan
  case
125 g (4 oz) frozen
  blackberries,
  thawed

Beat the cheese and yogurt together until smooth. Add the vanilla essence, honey and lemon juice and beat until thoroughly blended.

Spoon into the flan case and top with the blackberries. Chill before serving.

Serves 4

Moroccan Orange Salad

4 large or 6 medium
  oranges
50 g (2 oz) dates,
  roughly chopped
25 g (1 oz) flaked
  almonds
2 tablespoons caster
  sugar
juice of 2 lemons
ground cinnamon to
  decorate

Peel and slice the oranges, discarding
the pith. Place in a serving dish with
the dates and almonds.

Mix together the sugar and lemon
juice and pour over the fruit mixture.
Chill for at least 2 hours before
serving.

Sprinkle with cinnamon to taste.
Serve with cream, if liked.

Serves 4

Treacle Tart

1 x 212 g (7½ oz)
packet frozen
shortcrust pastry,
thawed
4 tablespoons
cornflakes,
crushed, or fresh
white breadcrumbs
6 tablespoons golden
syrup, warmed
juice of ½ lemon
½ teaspoon ground
ginger

Roll out the pastry and use to line a
20 cm (8 inch) ovenproof plate.
Trim, knock up the edge and flute.
Reserve the pastry trimmings. Prick
the pastry base.
  Sprinkle half the cornflakes or
breadcrumbs in the pastry case and
pour in the syrup. Sprinkle the
lemon juice over the syrup.
  Mix the ginger with the remaining
cornflakes or breadcrumbs and
sprinkle over the top. Cut strips
from the pastry trimmings and make
a lattice pattern over the tart.
  Cook in a preheated moderately
hot oven, 190°C (375°F), Gas Mark
5, for 30 minutes until the pastry is
crisp and golden. Serve hot or cold.
Serves 4

Orange Tart

1 x 212 g (7½ oz)
  packet frozen
  shortcrust pastry,
  thawed
2 oranges, thinly
  sliced
1 egg, beaten
50 g (2 oz) ground
  almonds
1 tablespoon sugar
2 tablespoons clear
  honey

Roll out the pastry and use to line a
20 cm (8 inch) flan dish. Prick the
base. Line with a piece of
greaseproof paper and dried beans.
Bake blind in a preheated moderately
hot oven, 190°C (375°F), Gas
Mark 5, for 15 minutes. Remove the
beans and paper.

Meanwhile, put the oranges in a
small pan. Add just enough water to
cover and simmer for about 30
minutes until the peel is tender.
Drain.

Beat together the egg, almonds
and sugar until smooth. Spread in
the flan case and arrange the orange
slices on top. Spoon over the honey.
Return to the oven for 20 minutes.

Serve hot or cold, with cream.
Serves 4

Stuffed Oranges

2 large oranges
1 dessert apple,
    peeled, cored and
    chopped
1 tablespoon raisins
1 tablespoon chopped
    dates
1 tablespoon
    hazelnuts, toasted
    and chopped
1 tablespoon soft
    brown sugar
120 ml (4 fl oz)
    double cream
1 teaspoon icing
    sugar
orange twists to
    decorate (optional)

Halve the oranges and scoop out the flesh, keeping the shells intact; set aside.

Chop the orange flesh, discarding all pith, and place in a bowl. Add the apple, raisins, dates, nuts and brown sugar. Mix well and pile into the orange halves.

Whip the cream with the icing sugar until it forms soft peaks. Spoon on top of the oranges. Chill before serving, decorated with orange twists if liked.
Serves 4

Apple Toffee Dessert

1 medium cooking
    apple, peeled,
    cored and chopped
1 large dessert apple,
    peeled, cored and
    chopped
50 g (2 oz) demerara
    or soft brown
    sugar
50 g (2 oz) butter
juice of 1/2 lemon
2 slices stale white
    bread, crusts
    removed, cut into
    cubes
4 tablespoons double
    cream, lightly
    whipped

Sprinkle the apples with the sugar and toss well to coat evenly.

Melt half the butter in a frying pan, add the apple and fry quickly until just soft. Transfer to a warmed serving dish, using a slotted spoon. Sprinkle with the lemon juice and keep warm.

Melt the remaining butter in the pan, add the bread cubes and fry, turning, until crisp and evenly golden.

Add the bread to the apple pieces and mix well. Serve immediately, topped with whipped cream.
Serves 4

Citrus Trifles

4 trifle sponges
2 tablespoons
   Cointreau
2 oranges
3 tablespoons lemon
   curd
2 egg whites
4 lemon twists to
   decorate

Put the trifle sponges in 4 individual glass dishes and sprinkle with the Cointreau.

Peel the oranges, removing all pith, and chop roughly. Divide between the trifle sponges.

Put the lemon curd in a bowl. Whisk the egg whites until stiff and fold into the lemon curd. Spoon over the orange pieces.

Decorate with lemon twists. Chill before serving.

Serves 4

Chocolate Mousse

175 g (6 oz) cooking
   chocolate, broken
   into pieces
3 tablespoons strong
   black coffee
1 tablespoon brandy
4 eggs, separated
TO DECORATE:
150 ml (¼ pint)
   double cream,
   whipped
flaked almonds,
   toasted

Put the chocolate, coffee and brandy
in a bowl over a saucepan of hot
water and stir until melted. Remove
from the heat and leave to cool for
1 minute.

Add the egg yolks to the chocolate
mixture and beat well. Whisk the
egg whites until stiff and fold into
the chocolate mixture.

Pour into a soufflé dish and chill
for at least 3 hours before serving.
Decorate with whipped cream and
almonds.
Serves 4

Butterscotch Nut Pie

25 g (1 oz) butter
6 digestive biscuits,
  crushed
200 ml (1/3 pint) milk
120 ml (4 fl oz)
  single cream
1 x 68 g (3 oz)
  packet butterscotch
  quick whip
50 g (2 oz)
  hazelnuts, toasted
  and chopped
TO DECORATE:
150 ml (1/4 pint)
  double cream,
  whipped
hazelnuts, toasted

Melt the butter and stir in the biscuit crumbs. Press into the base of a 15 cm (6 inch) flan dish.

Gradually add the milk and cream to the butterscotch whip, mixing until smooth. Add the hazelnuts and pile on top of the biscuit base.

Decorate with whipped cream and hazelnuts just before serving.

Serves 4

Pears en Compote

1 x 539 g (19 oz)
  can pear halves
300 ml (½ pint) red
  wine
2 teaspoons ground
  cinnamon
50 g (2 oz) dates,
  chopped

Drain the pears, reserving 150 ml
(¼ pint) of the juice. Place the pears,
wine, reserved pear juice and
cinnamon in a pan. Bring to the boil,
then lower the heat, cover and
simmer for 10 minutes.

Add the dates, remove from the
heat and leave to cool. Serve chilled,
with cream if liked.

Serves 4

Baked Bananas

50 g (2 oz) butter
2 tablespoons soft
    brown sugar
2 tablespoons lemon
    juice
4 bananas
2 tablespoons brandy

Put the butter, sugar and lemon juice in a shallow casserole. Place in a preheated moderate oven, 180°C (350°F), Gas Mark 4, for a few minutes until melted.

Cut the bananas into large pieces and arrange in the casserole, turning to coat with the sauce. Add the brandy, cover and return to the oven for 30 minutes.

Serve piping hot, accompanied by single cream.

Serves 4

Ginger Rum Trifle

1 x 227 g (8 oz)
   ginger cake, sliced
1 x 212 g (7½ oz)
   can pear quarters
6 tablespoons rum
300 ml (½ pint) cold
   thick custard
150 ml (¼ pint)
   double cream
1-2 teaspoons icing
   sugar
flaked almonds,
   toasted, to decorate

Line a medium soufflé dish or glass
bowl with half the ginger cake.
   Drain the pears, reserving
2 tablespoons of the juice. Mix the
rum with the reserved pear juice and
sprinkle half over the cake. Place the
pears on top, cover with the
remaining cake and pour over the
remaining rum mixture.
   Spoon the custard over the cake.
Whip the cream with the icing sugar
until it forms soft peaks. Spoon over
the custard and decorate with
almonds.
Serves 4

Caledonian Cream

3 tablespoons ginger
    marmalade
250 ml (8 fl oz)
    double cream
3 tablespoons caster
    sugar
2 tablespoons whisky
2 tablespoons lemon
    juice
2 egg whites
soft brown or
    demerara sugar to
    decorate

Divide the marmalade between
4 individual glass dishes.

Whip the cream until stiff, then
fold in the caster sugar, whisky and
lemon juice. Whisk the egg whites
until stiff and fold into the cream
mixture.

Spoon the cream mixture over the
marmalade and sprinkle with brown
sugar to decorate.

Serves 4

Ginger Log

24 ginger snaps
4 tablespoons rum
450 ml (³/4 pint)
  double cream
1½ teaspoons ground
  ginger
1½ tablespoons
  caster sugar
1½ tablespoons
  ginger syrup (from
  stem ginger)
stem ginger slices to
  decorate

Place the biscuits in a shallow dish and sprinkle with the rum. Leave until completely absorbed.

Whip the cream with the ground ginger and sugar until stiff. Fold in the ginger syrup.

Sandwich all the biscuits together, using two-thirds of the cream, to make a long roll. Place on a serving dish and cover with the remaining cream. Decorate with the stem ginger.

Serves 4

Port and Prune Fool

284 ml (10 fl oz)
  double cream
1 x 439 g (15½ oz)
  can prunes, stoned
4 tablespoons port
50 g (2 oz) soft
  brown sugar
grated nutmeg
chopped nuts to
  decorate

Whip the cream until stiff. Chop the prunes and fold into the cream with the port, sugar and nutmeg to taste.

Spoon into individual glass dishes and chill. Decorate with chopped nuts before serving.

Serves 4

Mont Blanc Meringues

120 ml (4 fl oz)
  double cream
1 x 227 g (8 oz) can
  sweetened chestnut
  purée
2 tablespoons Grand
  Marnier
8 meringue nests
flaked almonds,
  toasted, to decorate

Whip the cream until stiff, then fold half into the chestnut purée with the Grand Marnier.

Pile the chestnut cream into the meringue nests. Swirl the remaining cream on top to resemble a snow-capped peak. Decorate with almonds. Serve immediately.

Serves 4

Iced Chocolate Mint Meringues

25 g (1 oz) plain
   chocolate, chopped
4 portions soft
   vanilla ice cream
8 meringue nests
4 tablespoons crème
   de menthe or
   Royal mint
   chocolate liqueur
grated chocolate to
   decorate (optional)

Fold the chocolate into the ice cream
and spoon a portion into each
meringue nest. Sprinkle the liqueur
over the top. Decorate with grated
chocolate if liked. Serve
immediately.

Serves 4

NOTE: As a variation, use chopped
peppermint chocolate sticks instead
of plain chocolate.

Puerto Rican Coffee Ice

1 x 212 g (7½ oz)
  can peach slices,
  drained
4 tablespoons Tia
  Maria or Grand
  Marnier
75 g (3 oz)
  granulated sugar
2 tablespoons water
75 g (3 oz) flaked
  almonds, toasted
4 portions coffee ice
  cream

Divide the peach slices between 4 glass dishes, sprinkle with the liqueur and set aside.

Place the sugar and water in a small pan over low heat until dissolved, then boil steadily for 3 to 4 minutes until the syrup turns light brown. Immediately stir in the almonds and pour onto an oiled baking sheet. Leave to cool, then break the praline into pieces.

Place a portion of ice cream in each serving dish and top with the praline. Serve immediately.
Serves 4

INDEX